11+
VERBAL REASONING

Series editor Tracey Phelps,
the 11+ tutor with a

96% PASS RATE

ges 9–10

ractice

■SCHOLASTIC

Published in the UK by Scholastic Education, 2021

Book End, Range Road, Witney, Oxfordshire, OX29 0YD

A division of Scholastic Limited

London – New York – Toronto – Sydney – Auckland

Mexico City – New Delhi – Hong Kong

SCHOLASTIC and associated logos are trademarks and/or registered trademarks of Scholastic Inc.

www.scholastic.co.uk

1 2 3 4 5 6 7 8 9   1 2 3 4 5 6 7 8 9 0

British Library Cataloguing-in-Publication Data

A catalogue record for this book is available from the British Library.

ISBN 978-1407-19021-1

Printed and bound by Ashford Colour Press Ltd.

Papers used by Scholastic Limited are made from wood grown in sustainable forests.

Author

Tracey Phelps

Editorial team

Vicki Yates, Sarah Davies, Julia Roberts

Design team

Dipa Mistry, Andrea Lewis and Couper Street Type Co.

Contents

About the CEM test and this book 4

Spelling 5

Synonyms 9

Antonyms 13

Synonyms: missing letters 17

Antonyms: missing letters 21

Synonyms: the odd one out 25

Vocabulary revision 29

Vocabulary: matching words and their definitions 33

Making words 37

Cloze passages 42

Shuffled sentences 48

Answers 54

About the CEM test

About the CEM test and this book

The Centre for Evaluation and Monitoring (CEM) is one of the leading providers of the tests that grammar schools use in selecting students at 11+. The CEM test assesses a student's ability in Verbal Reasoning, Non-verbal Reasoning, English and Mathematics. Pupils typically take the CEM test at the start of Year 6.

Students answer multiple-choice questions and record their answers on a separate answer sheet. This answer sheet is then marked via OMR (Optical Mark Recognition) scanning technology.

The content and question types may vary slightly each year. The English and Verbal Reasoning components have included synonyms, antonyms, word associations, shuffled sentences, cloze (gap fill) passages and comprehension questions.

The Mathematics and Non-verbal Reasoning components span the Key Stage 2 Mathematics curriculum, with emphasis on worded problems. It is useful to note that the CEM test may include Mathematics topics introduced at Year 6, such as ratio, proportion and probability.

The other main provider of such tests is GL Assessment. The GLA test assesses the same subjects as the CEM test and uses a multiple-choice format.

About this book

Scholastic 11+ Verbal Reasoning for the CEM test (ages 9–10) is part of the Pass Your 11+ series and offers authentic multiple-choice practice activities.

This book offers:

- Targeted practice and opportunities for children to test their understanding and develop their verbal reasoning skills.

- Opportunities to master different question types including cloze, spelling, vocabulary, synonyms, antonyms and more.

- Multiple-choice questions that reflect the different question types that are common in the CEM 11+ test, at a level appropriate for the age group.

- Short answers at the end of the book.

- Extended answers online with useful explanations at **www.scholastic.co.uk/pass-your-11-plus/extras** or via the QR code opposite.

How to use this book

It is suggested that your child focuses on one question type at a time and that they practise in regular bite-size chunks of time (e.g. 20 minutes). As your child becomes more proficient, reduce the time allowed but expect the same number of questions to be covered in order to practise working at speed.

Your child's scores in each section will allow you to see where their strengths lie and areas where they might need more practice in the future.

Spelling

In the following sentences there are some spelling mistakes. On each line there is either one mistake or no mistakes. Find the group of words with the mistake in it and circle the letter. If there is no mistakes, circle the N in the box on the right.

1. Sonia felt lucky to have such a leniant teacher.
   A   B   C   D   N

2. The soup was far too spicey for my liking; I prefer things to taste bland.
   A   B   C   D   N

3. Stella's principle reason for moving house was that her neighbours were noisy.
   A   B   C   D   N

4. William savered his breakfast, which was served to him in bed on Father's Day.
   A   B   C   D   N

5. The family ploughed on threw the woods until they found somewhere for their tent.
   A   B   C   D   N

6. Richard was still not entirely certain who's pen he had borrowed.
   A   B   C   D   N

7. It was only a miner mistake, but Amina's teacher was livid.
   A   B   C   D   N

8. Mahin was thrilled to have been given the starring roll in the school play.
   A   B   C   D   N

9. The builders raised the old barn to the ground before laying foundations for a house.
   A   B   C   D   N

10. Although she followed quite a plane and simple recipe, the cake was a disaster.
    A   B   C   D   N

11. Annie worked hard to establish her own business and she was ultimately successful.
    A   B   C   D   N

12. Martin's mussels were aching after he had spent the entire morning at the gym.
    A   B   C   D   N

13. As Alanna walked home from the cinema, she was concious that she needed to hurry.
    A   B   C   D   N

/13

14 Matt's curiousity was aroused when he noticed his neighbour's new car.

| A | B | C | D |

N

15 As it was such a pleasant afternoon, Gus's teacher decided to take lessens outside.

| A | B | C | D |

N

16 Sree was regretting agreeing to be part of the local planning commitee.

| A | B | C | D |

N

17 Bethan's grandparents were celebrating being married for fourty years.

| A | B | C | D |

N

18 She couldn't put her finger on it exactly, but Si sensed something wierd was afoot.

| A | B | C | D |

N

19 Thomas couldn't wait to start attending bording school in September.

| A | B | C | D |

N

20 After arriving at their holiday destination, Jon was desperate to get onto the beech.

| A | B | C | D |

N

21 Emma bought a new summer skirt, but she had to make some altarations to it.

| A | B | C | D |

N

22 Class 6T were all asked to read a novel and write a book revue by Friday.

| A | B | C | D |

N

23 Clara took her twins to their favourite liesure centre for advanced diving classes.

| A | B | C | D |

N

24 Sunil was truely captivated by the sight of the Taj Mahal on his trip to India.

| A | B | C | D |

N

25 Paula got hopelessly lost on the journey as she was unfamilar with the route.

| A | B | C | D |

N

26 Erik was crossing off the days on his calendar; he couldn't wait for his birthday.

| A | B | C | D |

N

27 Patrick noticed that there were cracks in the sealing in the bathroom.

| A | B | C | D |

N

28 Erica used a brand-new pallet on which to mix her oil paints.

| A | B | C | D |

N

29 Joe's voice was really quite horse after he had been shouting instructions all day.

| A | B | C | D |

N

/16

30 Martha rung out the towel before carefully pegging it out on the washing line.

| A | B | C | D | | N |

31 Although he missed the start of the conversation, Jack got the jist of the story.

| A | B | C | D | | N |

32 Aran wasn't sure of the sauce of the gossip, but he was anxious to quash the rumour.

| A | B | C | D | | N |

33 Ella's knowledge of wildlife was extremely limited, but she knew about hedgehogs.

| A | B | C | D | | N |

34 Anna was looking forward to leading a more independant lifestyle at university.

| A | B | C | D | | N |

35 Sunita was desperately seeking some sensible advise on gardening.

| A | B | C | D | | N |

36 Luiz assured his parents that he would definately finish his homework on time.

| A | B | C | D | | N |

37 Lucy spent hours cooking delicious deserts for a dinner party for her friends.

| A | B | C | D | | N |

38 Liam was so vane; he spent hours looking in the mirror each day.

| A | B | C | D | | N |

39 Mum insisted that Ellie put her clothes on hangars, rather than on the floor.

| A | B | C | D | | N |

40 Marta had wanted to be a politician ever since she was a teenager.

| A | B | C | D | | N |

41 The ponies in the field always nay whenever a car goes past our house.

| A | B | C | D | | N |

42 Simon was looking extremely pail one morning, so he made a doctor's appointment.

| A | B | C | D | | N |

43 Liam accidentally hit the curb when cycling, which resulted in a puncture.

| A | B | C | D | | N |

44 Bianca ordered steak for main course and a lemon moose for pudding.

| A | B | C | D | | N |

45 Richard was ashamed when his cat caught flees, so he took it to the vet.

| A | B | C | D | | N |

/16

46 Although she knew that they weren't a healthy option, Kim found cookies irresistable.

| A | B | C | D |

N

47 Daphne was devastated when she lost her job as a lollypop lady; she loved her work.

| A | B | C | D |

N

48 Daniel's school were raising funds to put towards a new sports pavilion.

| A | B | C | D |

N

49 Vanda was hugely embarassed to discover that she had locked herself out again.

| A | B | C | D |

N

50 The stain on her shirt was barely noticable, but Surita still refused to wear it.

| A | B | C | D |

N

51 All through the winter, Alfie struggled with an irritating and persistant cough.

| A | B | C | D |

N

52 Amy's grandfather was very particular and always hated sitting in a draft.

| A | B | C | D |

N

53 Even during a recession, Joe still managed to show a prophet from his business.

| A | B | C | D |

N

54 Latif was irritated when one of his peddles suddenly fell off his bicycle.

| A | B | C | D |

N

55 Ellen was not aloud to go into town on her own, although her friends were.

| A | B | C | D |

N

56 Ben was sick of being harrassed over the state of his bedroom.

| A | B | C | D |

N

57 Paulo has quite a high pain threshhold, but he screamed when he tumbled over.

| A | B | C | D |

N

58 We're not a particularly religous family, but we do go to church occasionally.

| A | B | C | D |

N

59 Lorna was disappointed not to have been voted onto the Board of Governors.

| A | B | C | D |

N

60 Due to unforseen circumstances, the school is going to have to close immediately.

| A | B | C | D |

N

/15

Synonyms

Circle the word which has the most similar meaning to the word on the left.

1	**immune**	polluted	protected	powerful	potent
2	**fair**	improving	immediate	imprecise	impartial
3	**coarse**	vague	vicious	vulgar	vain
4	**spoil**	pamper	prosper	purge	profit
5	**notify**	intend	entail	inform	acclaim
6	**likely**	loosely	liable	merely	only
7	**akin**	related	relaxed	rational	regular
8	**fatigued**	expectant	exhausted	expensive	extrovert
9	**jauntily**	aimfully	dutifully	fancifully	cheerfully
10	**envy**	jealousy	jeopardy	joviality	jollity
11	**amaze**	scare	scrounge	astound	amass
12	**jumpy**	slippery	catchy	wiggly	jittery
13	**lapsed**	exposed	expired	extreme	extinct
14	**mainly**	surely	merely	largely	lengthy
15	**wary**	conspicuous	conscious	contrary	suspicious
16	**makeshift**	temporary	trendy	totally	torrid
17	**imposing**	impressive	imperative	important	impartial
18	**love**	concern	affection	regard	emotion
19	**explosive**	voluntary	variable	vicious	volatile
20	**furious**	loved	lucid	livid	lively
21	**horrible**	glum	glib	gutsy	grim
22	**lined**	controlled	ruled	managed	handled
23	**devoted**	legal	lethal	loyal	level

/23

24	**join**	whinge	melt	move	merge
25	**aware**	mindful	careful	wishful	needful
26	**marvellous**	impossible	improbable	impassable	incredible
27	**journal**	schedule	diary	rota	library
28	**lately**	serenely	generally	recently	literally
29	**find**	loosen	liberate	linger	locate
30	**little**	diluted	diminutive	decorative	daunting
31	**maim**	injure	perjure	assure	measure
32	**understand**	confound	apprehend	comprehend	correspond
33	**modify**	appear	adjust	allay	avoid
34	**formula**	method	menu	memo	merger
35	**inspire**	magnify	measure	maximise	motivate
36	**spotted**	striped	dappled	clouded	silvery
37	**gloomy**	murky	mouldy	dusty	musty
38	**first**	final	initial	partial	earlier
39	**mutiny**	parade	procession	rebellion	conference
40	**bewilder**	modify	mortify	magnify	mystify
41	**haggle**	mediate	placate	negotiate	nominate
42	**moisture**	coolness	mould	dampness	mixture
43	**normally**	seldom	ordinarily	uniquely	frequently
44	**beginner**	gremlin	follower	rival	novice
45	**void**	invalid	exempt	excluded	exploited
46	**obstinate**	unsuitable	inactive	inflexible	incapable
47	**cover**	obscure	vague	ambiguous	faint
48	**barrier**	limit	crisis	obstacle	lack
49	**incident**	scene	arena	spectacle	occurrence

/26

50	**strangely**	madly	curiously	bitterly	irritably
51	**junction**	interval	interruption	intersection	interlude
52	**mundane**	musty	orderly	cautionary	ordinary
53	**sailor**	magician	mariner	mannequin	mutineer
54	**unpleasant**	scary	shaky	odious	devious
55	**unscented**	tasteless	distasteful	perfumed	odourless
56	**menacing**	treacherous	ominous	infamous	perilous
57	**omit**	examine	exceed	exclude	expand
58	**energy**	vision	vitality	tonic	boost
59	**opinion**	viewpoint	endpoint	checkpoint	viewfinder
60	**orderly**	problematic	domestic	systematic	masterly
61	**outfox**	outrun	outline	outstare	outsmart
62	**domineering**	overreaching	overbearing	binding	damaging
63	**oversee**	overlook	overcome	supersede	supervise
64	**magnificent**	splendid	paltry	pretty	impeccable
65	**parade**	charade	procession	performance	competition
66	**puzzle**	doubt	poster	enigma	sticker
67	**incomplete**	unfair	partial	biased	attached
68	**particular**	specific	reserved	authentic	accurate
69	**lasting**	enlightening	endearing	earnest	enduring
70	**persuasive**	impressive	conclusive	convincing	satisfactory
71	**placidly**	meekly	calmly	solidly	purely
72	**appeal**	plea	plot	post	plan
73	**quandary**	doubt	necessity	urgency	dilemma
74	**delayed**	leisurely	leading	overdue	gradual
75	**plunge**	sweep	splash	swoop	stoop

/26

76	**laughter**	myth	scorn	mirth	banter
77	**silhouette**	disguise	outline	display	posture
78	**participant**	opponent	winner	competitor	champion
79	**futile**	worthless	priceless	faultless	pointless
80	**pollute**	consume	contaminate	complete	conspire
81	**allowance**	admission	service	ration	return
82	**positive**	sure	stable	suitable	serious
83	**dangerous**	haphazard	disagreeable	desperate	perilous
84	**pause**	interject	wait	interfere	interact
85	**accurate**	precise	limited	complex	searching
86	**predict**	forewarn	forsake	forecast	forfeit
87	**favour**	pamper	praise	pursue	prefer
88	**absent**	mislaid	missing	neglected	flawed
89	**priceless**	splendid	superb	excessive	valuable
90	**buy**	provide	supply	purchase	plunder
91	**launch**	propose	propel	promise	portray
92	**forthright**	diplomatic	emotional	outspoken	sincere
93	**advance**	profit	predict	preview	progress
94	**proof**	evidence	clue	suggestion	solution
95	**conquer**	convey	connect	conserve	overcome
96	**probable**	slightly	likely	merely	nearly
97	**wealth**	audacity	positivity	prosperity	luxury
98	**interfere**	pry	spy	try	ply
99	**soon**	frequently	promptly	currently	presently
100	**stringent**	soft	strict	solemn	surly

/25

Antonyms

Circle the word which has the most opposite meaning to the word on the left.

1 broken	infirm	injured	intact	inspired
2 integrate	solidify	separate	shuffle	straighten
3 strict	lazy	livid	lavish	lenient
4 captivity	liberty	legacy	legend	licence
5 inconsiderate	cute	dear	kind	mild
6 pacify	advise	acknowledge	soothe	agitate
7 eminent	unwise	unknown	untied	uneasy
8 support	transition	oppose	emotion	donation
9 synthetic	neutral	national	natural	normal
10 selfish	genial	gentle	genuine	generous
11 horizontal	upfront	upcoming	upright	upbeat
12 novice	judge	wizard	advisor	veteran
13 abruptly	gradually	generally	greatly	gallantly
14 indulge	object	allow	abstain	endorse
15 absurd	responsible	reliable	regrettable	reasonable
16 acceptance	reaction	rejection	division	conclusion
17 factual	incisive	indolent	instinctive	inaccurate
18 alarming	reserved	reassuring	refreshing	resisting
19 pleasing	awesome	fulsome	irksome	handsome
20 proud	ashamed	articulate	aloof	aghast
21 respect	concern	contempt	control	context
22 cruelty	domination	friction	complexion	compassion
23 boring	carefree	cheerful	compelling	confined

/23

24	**anxious**	unconcerned	cowardly	crazed	unqualified
25	**confirmation**	impulse	deprivation	distress	denial
26	**named**	abnormal	anonymous	superfluous	detailed
27	**objection**	upheaval	disposal	approval	interval
28	**modern**	outdated	homely	shabby	dowdy
29	**complexity**	quality	capacity	simplicity	purity
30	**refusal**	conversion	consent	critic	concern
31	**upset**	confirm	conceal	console	confer
32	**damaging**	hurtful	humiliating	heavy	helpful
33	**hurry**	dwindle	dawdle	dribble	drizzle
34	**dear**	inactive	unimportant	inexpensive	adorable
35	**honestly**	deceitfully	tactfully	carefully	mindfully
36	**encode**	defraud	enrich	endow	decipher
37	**uncommitted**	disloyal	dedicated	consistent	decisive
38	**addition**	answer	assumption	deduction	opinion
39	**clumsy**	delicate	supple	graceful	tasteful
40	**delight**	displeasure	disaster	disgrace	distrust
41	**unintentional**	careful	deliberate	cautious	concerned
42	**compliment**	inform	injure	insult	ignore
43	**depart**	move	divert	restore	return
44	**poor**	prominent	prosperous	paltry	passive
45	**deprive**	submit	support	provide	appoint
46	**cheerfulness**	disturbance	distraction	desire	despair
47	**destruction**	creation	emission	eruption	attention
48	**worsen**	impair	improve	intensify	instruct
49	**encourage**	infer	determine	deter	prefer

/26

50	**ailing**	hefty	healthy	heavy	haughty
51	**shy**	certain	assertive	poised	believing
52	**bright**	dirty	damp	dodgy	dingy
53	**pollute**	consume	corrupt	cleanse	soak
54	**vanish**	commence	occur	proceed	emerge
55	**connected**	detached	demotivated	disposed	disputed
56	**dispatch**	return	repeat	receive	repeal
57	**conceal**	cover	disclose	disable	distract
58	**rude**	critical	courageous	casual	courteous
59	**faithful**	disobedient	discontented	disloyal	dishonest
60	**satisfied**	resentful	displeased	disturbed	discounted
61	**divide**	simplify	classify	unify	amplify
62	**certain**	unlikely	absurd	secure	unnatural
63	**fill**	drop	ease	bloat	drain
64	**easy**	tolerant	demanding	flexible	elaborate
65	**economical**	hasty	sloppy	wasteful	spoiled
66	**lower**	appoint	elevate	hustle	shove
67	**confuse**	commute	compare	corrode	clarify
68	**endanger**	prolong	protest	protect	prefer
69	**limited**	endless	abrupt	edited	defined
70	**sluggish**	magnetic	energetic	lethargic	diplomatic
71	**ignorant**	enriched	enlightened	enraged	encouraged
72	**exactly**	coarsely	rudely	bluntly	roughly
73	**save**	sneer	simmer	squander	splatter
74	**experienced**	unsuitable	unskilled	unlikely	uncertain
75	**insert**	resolve	relax	extract	renew

/26

76	**extreme**	pleasant	moderate	sparing	detached
77	**genuine**	framed	feared	flawed	forged
78	**feeble**	fretful	faithful	powerful	peaceful
79	**flood**	draught	danger	defence	drought
80	**following**	afterward	previous	backward	gathering
81	**cheerful**	fanciful	fawning	forlorn	futile
82	**fresh**	stale	stark	solid	slimy
83	**eager**	unfeeling	excited	unfailing	unwilling
84	**general**	different	inexact	specific	vague
85	**delightful**	grumpy	disagreeable	ghostly	greatly
86	**calm**	bitter	burning	binding	blustery
87	**release**	relay	remain	retain	repel
88	**decisive**	uncertain	unafraid	unnerved	unshaken
89	**quiet**	harsh	brusque	boisterous	buoyant
90	**attach**	unload	unblock	uncover	unfasten
91	**reality**	frivolity	fantasy	folly	fraud
92	**dry**	hardy	hefty	humid	husky
93	**unlikely**	practical	preferable	preventable	probable
94	**random**	accidental	radical	methodical	mechanical
95	**inappropriate**	adaptable	suitable	adorable	enviable
96	**basic**	complicated	furtive	forlorn	familiar
97	**constant**	uncertain	changeable	cheating	compatible
98	**essential**	special	unsuccessful	unhelpful	unnecessary
99	**formal**	unofficial	unsocial	material	ceremonial
100	**involve**	examine	exclude	express	extract

/25

Synonyms: missing letters

Complete the word on the right to have a similar meaning to the word on the left.

1 immaculate — f _ a _ _ e s s

2 huge — _ m m _ _ s e

3 creative — i _ _ e n _ i v e

4 magnificent — s _ u _ _ i n g

5 guess — _ s t _ m _ t e

6 astonishing — _ m a _ _ n g

7 storm — _ e m _ _ s t

8 impulse — i _ _ t i _ c t

9 victory — t _ i _ m _ h

10 appropriate — _ u _ t _ b l e

11 surprised — s _ _ r _ l e d

12 disbelieving — d _ _ b _ f u l

13 prohibited — _ a n n _ _

/13

14	boring	t _ _ i o _ s
15	ultimate	_ i _ _ l
16	terrible	a _ p _ l _ i n g
17	meticulous	t h _ _ _ u g h
18	flourishing	_ h r _ v i n _
19	annoying	_ r r _ t _ t i n g
20	tolerable	b _ _ r _ b l e
21	wobble	t _ _ m _ l e
22	truancy	a _ s _ _ c e
23	violent	t u _ _ _ l e n t
24	thanks	g _ a _ i t u _ e
25	unbeatable	i n _ i n c _ b _ e
26	credible	b _ _ _ e v a b l e
27	undecided	u n _ _ r _ a i n
28	urge	p _ _ _ s _ a d e
29	absolutely	u t _ e _ l y

/16

30	defeat	c _ _ q _ e r
31	varied	a _ _ o _ t e d
32	hugely	v _ _ t l _
33	vicious	s a _ _ g _
34	journey	v _ _ a _ e
35	remove	w _ t _ d _ a w
36	worn	s _ a _ _ y
37	about	r o _ g _ l _
38	suddenly	a _ r _ p t _ y
39	adapt	_ d _ u _ t
40	acquire	_ b _ a _ n
41	stick	a _ h _ _ e
42	vital	c _ i _ i c _ l
43	admitted	c _ n _ e _ s e d
44	loveable	a _ _ r a _ l e
45	height	a _ t _ t _ d e

/16

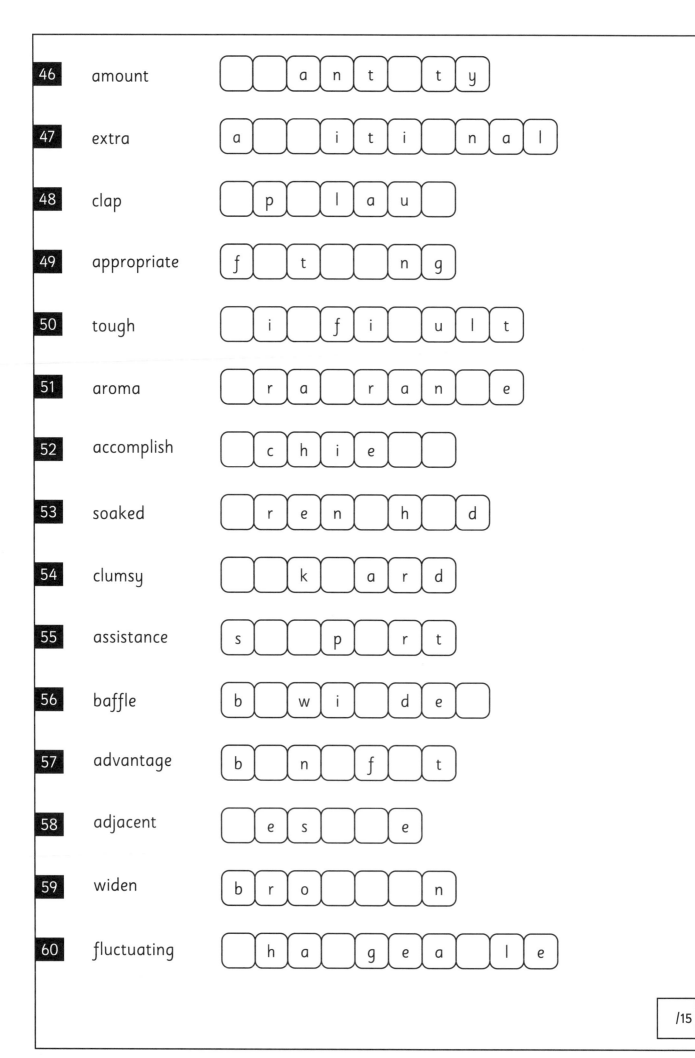

46	amount	☐ ☐ a n t ☐ t y
47	extra	a ☐ ☐ i t i ☐ n a l
48	clap	☐ p ☐ l a u ☐
49	appropriate	f ☐ t ☐ ☐ n g
50	tough	☐ i ☐ f i ☐ u l t
51	aroma	☐ r a ☐ r a n ☐ e
52	accomplish	☐ c h i e ☐ ☐
53	soaked	☐ r e n ☐ h ☐ d
54	clumsy	☐ ☐ k ☐ a r d
55	assistance	s ☐ ☐ p ☐ r t
56	baffle	b ☐ w i ☐ d e ☐
57	advantage	b ☐ n ☐ f ☐ t
58	adjacent	☐ e s ☐ ☐ e
59	widen	b r o ☐ ☐ ☐ n
60	fluctuating	☐ h a ☐ g e a ☐ l e

/15

Antonyms: missing letters

Complete the word on the right to have an opposite meaning to the word on the left.

1. disappoint   i _ _ r e s _

2. insufficient   _ d e _ u a t _

3. incapable   c o _ p e t _ _ t

4. remove   i _ _ _ a l l

5. establish   a _ _ _ i s h

6. unite   s e _ _ r _ t e

7. hidden   _ _ s i b l _

8. jovial   m i _ _ _ a b l e

9. keen   r e l _ _ t _ n t

10. effortless   s _ r e _ u _ u s

11. leisurely   _ u r r _ _ d

12. safe   l _ _ h _ l

13. stable   _ l i m _ _

/13

14	frequently	s c ☐ ☐ ☐ e l y
15	slowly	r a ☐ ☐ ☐ l y
16	cautiously	r ☐ ☐ h ☐ y
17	inferiority	☐ u ☐ l ☐ t ☐
18	destroy	☐ e b u i ☐ ☐
19	recede	a ☐ ☐ a n c ☐
20	deteriorate	i ☐ p ☐ o ☐ e
21	repel	a ☐ ☐ r a ☐ t
22	accept	r ☐ ☐ i s ☐
23	revolting	p ☐ ☐ a s a ☐ t
24	boring	g ☐ i p ☐ i ☐ g
25	approximate	☐ x ☐ ☐ t
26	artificial	☐ ☐ t u r ☐ l
27	foolishness	w i ☐ ☐ ☐ m
28	abandon	s ☐ l v ☐ g ☐
29	different	i ☐ e n ☐ ☐ c a l

/16

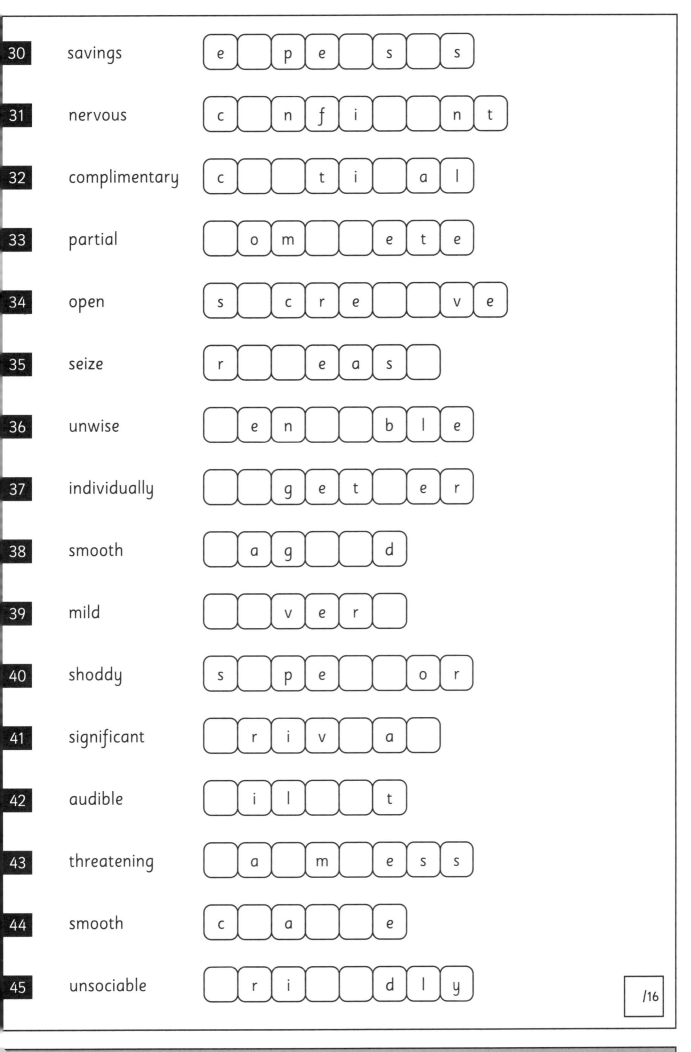

30	savings	e _ p e _ s _ s
31	nervous	c _ n f i _ _ n t
32	complimentary	c _ _ t i _ a l
33	partial	_ o m _ _ e t e
34	open	s _ c r e _ _ v e
35	seize	r _ _ e a s _
36	unwise	_ e n _ _ b l e
37	individually	_ _ g e t _ e r
38	smooth	_ a g _ _ d
39	mild	_ _ v e r _
40	shoddy	s _ p e _ _ o r
41	significant	_ r i v _ a _
42	audible	_ i l _ _ _ t
43	threatening	_ a m _ e s s
44	smooth	c _ a _ _ e
45	unsociable	_ r i _ _ d l y

/16

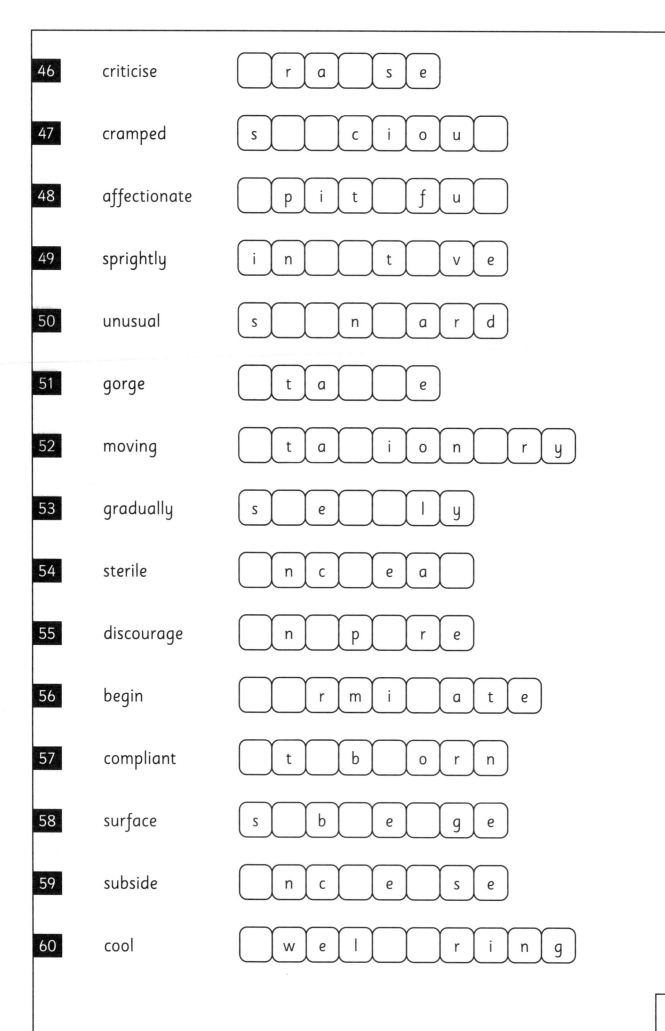

46	criticise	_ r a _ s e
47	cramped	s _ _ c i o u _
48	affectionate	_ p i t _ f u _
49	sprightly	i n _ _ t _ v e
50	unusual	s _ _ n _ a r d
51	gorge	_ t a _ _ e
52	moving	_ t a _ i o n _ r y
53	gradually	s _ e _ _ l y
54	sterile	_ n c _ e a _
55	discourage	_ n _ p _ r e
56	begin	_ _ r m i _ a t e
57	compliant	_ t _ b _ o r n
58	surface	s _ b _ e _ g e
59	subside	_ n c _ e _ s e
60	cool	_ w e l _ _ r i n g

/15

Antonyms: missing letters

Synonyms: the odd one out

Circle the word which is the odd one out.

1	idea	notion	attention	thought
2	narrative	diary	story	tale
3	impartial	unbiased	vague	neutral
4	standard	ordinary	special	general
5	novelist	writer	author	collector
6	imaginary	genuine	fictional	unreal
7	refuge	haven	habitat	sanctuary
8	brawl	scrap	oddment	remnant
9	traditional	conventional	customary	cursory
10	laborious	strenuous	ominous	arduous
11	cord	twine	rope	tangle
12	overhaul	renovate	replay	revamp
13	polite	astute	courteous	respectful
14	frayed	fractured	torn	ripped
15	ration	quota	allowance	distribution
16	wallow	enjoy	delight	revel
17	reasonable	thoughtful	sensible	logical
18	wilful	baleful	obstinate	stubborn
19	change	rectify	correct	remedy
20	regular	orderly	normal	usual
21	answer	reply	report	respond
22	legal	legitimate	linear	lawful
23	likeness	resemblance	similarity	solidarity

/23

24	admired	abashed	respected	esteemed
25	responsive	alert	aware	acute
26	incentive	motivation	prevention	reason
27	restrict	limit	confine	select
28	vengeance	revenge	retaliation	jealousy
29	dither	wander	waver	hesitate
30	level	flat	equal	even
31	twitter	wander	roam	ramble
32	rogue	scoundrel	rebel	rascal
33	rotund	obtuse	stout	plump
34	ban	refuse	waste	rubbish
35	permit	consent	allow	perform
36	shrewd	shrill	astute	smart
37	scamper	scuttle	strike	dash
38	locate	explore	uncover	unearth
39	danger	peril	trial	jeopardy
40	disperse	disrupt	scatter	dispel
41	bowl	ladle	scoop	spoon
42	amplify	enlarge	modify	magnify
43	scold	scorch	singe	burn
44	opponent	competition	contest	match
45	meadow	hedge	pasture	field
46	examine	exceed	analyse	inspect
47	shield	defend	squander	protect
48	mixture	blend	combination	variety
49	disgraceful	credulous	scandalous	shameful

/26

Synonyms: the odd one out

50	oval	rhombus	circle	crescent
51	incompetent	incomplete	useless	incapable
52	recreation	remorse	enjoyment	pleasure
53	calmness	serenity	immunity	tranquillity
54	memorise	recall	remember	recollect
55	sincere	honest	modest	earnest
56	devise	design	diagram	drawing
57	solace	comfort	convenience	consolation
58	revolve	rotate	spin	split
59	scour	spray	scrub	scrape
60	status	position	part	rank
61	tense	nervous	anxious	serious
62	tempo	rhyme	pace	speed
63	squabble	scribble	bicker	quarrel
64	scarcely	bizarrely	strangely	curiously
65	strict	stern	stringent	stark
66	propose	engage	recommend	suggest
67	shady	swampy	boggy	marshy
68	swear	promote	promise	pledge
69	present	gift	talent	flair
70	tamper	interfere	trample	meddle
71	entice	ensnare	coax	tempt
72	solemn	sombre	prim	glum
73	subject	discussion	topic	theme
74	idea	opinion	view	vista
75	push	crush	squash	flatten

/26

76	twitter	chirp	cheep	flutter
77	veer	brake	steer	swerve
78	vendor	customer	seller	trader
79	summary	verdict	judgement	decision
80	energy	vitality	vivacity	agility
81	observant	obedient	vigilant	watchful
82	wealth	affluence	luxury	prosperity
83	worldly	wholly	completely	entirely
84	wreckage	debris	carnage	rubble
85	vain	arrogant	concerned	conceited
86	charge	modify	change	adapt
87	ado	fuss	care	bother
88	irate	baffled	enraged	livid
89	inform	notify	advise	enrich
90	arguable	inevitable	debatable	disputable
91	badge	emblem	award	crest
92	shy	sly	coy	bashful
93	irksome	gruesome	irritating	annoying
94	bowl	throw	slide	hurl
95	brittle	peculiar	delicate	fragile
96	bustle	burst	puncture	rupture
97	hurry	splash	dash	scurry
98	cheerful	grateful	blithe	pleased
99	order	reserve	command	instruct
100	fascinating	compelling	gruelling	gripping

/25

Vocabulary revision

Substitute the words or phrases in bold with a word from the box below. Write the correct letter in each box on the right.

A imagine	**E** obedient	**I** fit	**M** tolerant	**Q** exhausted
B perfect	**F** decided	**J** innocent	**N** oppose	**R** manage
C opening	**G** overjoyed	**K** location	**O** survivors	**S** certain
D monitor	**H** investigate	**L** ignore	**P** resemble	**T** illustrate

1 Sadly, the rescue party found very few **people still alive**.

2 Harish **made up his mind** to go to the cinema on Saturday rather than Sunday.

3 Sophie's parents take plenty of exercise and are always **in very good shape**.

4 Betsy's cat found a small **gap** in the fence and managed to escape.

5 Aron's teacher asked him to make up a poem and **add a drawing to** it.

6 Freddie decided that he would **pay no attention to** his sister's moaning.

7 Emilie could never **think of** a world without the internet.

8 The defendant tried to convince the judge that he was **not guilty**.

9 The police needed to **make some inquiries about** the cause of the accident.

10 The rescued sailors were wet and hungry, and looked **haggard**.

11 Alina's parents are both very **easy-going**.

12 Both Kieran and Daniel **look like** their dad.

13 Halima had always wanted to **be in charge of** her own business.

14 Jamil's pet dog was always **well behaved**.

15 After her stay in hospital, Millie was advised to **keep an eye on** her temperature.

16 No one in the family dares to **stand up to** Aunt Amy.

17 When you buy something new, you can expect it to be **flawless**.

18 Lucy knew the perfect **place** for a family picnic.

19 Hari was **thrilled** to have passed his driving test first time.

20 Lidia was **positive** that she had everything she needed for her school trip.

/20

A forgetful	**E** saturated	**I** novelist	**M** grotesque	**Q** withered
B unwell	**F** shocked	**J** rotate	**N** sufficient	**R** thirsty
C practical	**G** unemployed	**K** outrun	**O** speechless	**S** ambition
D disorganised	**H** accustomed to	**L** vacant	**P** naive	**T** valuable

21 Matilda is a very **down-to-earth** sort of person, and she is always well organised.

22 Emma was anxious about whether she would have **enough** food for the party.

23 Bendek's daffodils **wilted** because he couldn't be bothered to water them.

24 Archie's jeans were **wet through** after he fell into the pond.

25 The Taylors owned a mouldy old flat which had been **unoccupied** for years.

26 Even though Ben had new shelves in his bedroom, his books were still **muddled**.

27 Ingrid blew nearly all of her annual bonus on a brand-new, superfast **expensive** car.

28 Ava's dad is **out of work** at the moment and is frantically looking for a new job.

29 Freddie had his tablet confiscated; he had been caught calling his little sister **ugly**.

30 As Larry watched yet another ready meal **go round** in the microwave, he wished that he had learned to cook lovely homemade dinners.

31 Ana's granny seems to be so **absent-minded** lately – last week she completely forgot where she had parked her car.

32 Cyrek is so **used to** the mess in his bedroom, he hardly notices it now.

33 Abbie's **aim** is to become a best-selling author.

34 Mahib was very **easily taken in** when he bought a second-hand car; it had all sorts of mechanical problems and it broke down several times.

35 J.K. Rowling is a very successful and famous **writer of fiction**.

36 Stella was feeling **off colour** on Monday morning, so she decided to stay at home.

37 An antelope can easily **move faster than** a lion.

38 George was somewhat **taken by surprise** when his train arrived on time.

39 After the match, the teams were desperately **longing for a drink**.

40 Nadia was **lost for words** when Arjun said that he had left his phone on the bus.

/20

A nimble	**E** blonde	**I** criticise	**M** always	**Q** improving
B afford	**F** leave	**J** monitoring	**N** miserable	**R** discovered
C conceal	**G** dare	**K** dusting	**O** modify	**S** cheap
D concentrate	**H** arrogant	**L** entry	**P** choice	**T** ajar

41 Mike was **keeping track of** events on an online blog. ☐

42 After landing an exciting new job, things were **looking up** for Alice. ☐

43 Sofia tried to **cover up** the fact that she had cracked the screen on her phone. ☐

44 Oliver had begun to get **above himself** after he won the Footballer of the Year award again. ☐

45 Although Tom's granny is 85, she is still very **sprightly** for her age. ☐

46 Poppy always likes to sleep with her bedroom door **slightly open**. ☐

47 When the river flooded our village, we had to **abandon** our house. ☐

48 Petra wanted to **adapt** her bike to make it go faster. ☐

49 **Admission** to the music festival is free for children. ☐

50 I can't **find the money for** a new pair of boots at the moment. ☐

51 Noah is **invariably** late when picking Patrick and Rosey up from school. ☐

52 Alfie has ginger hair and his sister, Lucy, is **fair-haired**. ☐

53 Copies of Minecraft are quite **moderately priced** at the moment. ☐

54 There was a massive **selection** of puddings at the restaurant. ☐

55 Zina was finding it hard to **pay attention** during a very boring talk from the head teacher. ☐

56 Katie was excited when she woke up to find a **sprinkling** of snow covering the garden. ☐

57 Luna was reluctant to **find fault with** Kai's homemade cupcakes, but they weren't really properly cooked in the middle. ☐

58 Would you **have the nerve** to sleep in a house that is rumoured to be haunted? ☐

59 Ruby was really disappointed when she **became aware** that Max had not been handing in his homework on time. ☐

60 Kasinda always seems to be so **down in the dumps**. ☐

/20

A airy	E baffled	I authorise	M omit	Q undecided
B honest	F crucial	J sparkling	N answer	R cosy
C blundered	G lovable	K remain	O assistance	S opposed
D unenthusiastic	H alter	L assortment	P accelerate	T3 toxic

61 Dave tried hard to **stay** calm when he discovered that his daughter had got a tattoo.

62 The vast majority of people are decent and **law-abiding**.

63 Patsy was **in two minds about** whether she liked the main course.

64 The marathon runners began to **go faster** as they rounded the last bend on the course.

65 The Board of Governors has to **approve** any plans to alter the school timetable.

66 Nathan knew that his next move would be **vitally important**.

67 Abbas was convinced that the deserted house held the **key** to solving the mystery.

68 Lucy was feeling somewhat **half-hearted** about her trip to see a Shakespeare play.

69 Granny's cottage has a really lovely, **homely** feel.

70 Some mushrooms can be **poisonous**, so don't pick them.

71 Mr Thomas asked his class all to read the same book, but to **leave out** Chapter 2.

72 Jakob's dad visited the pet rescue centre and returned home with a **delightful** kitten.

73 Jake's grandfather walks with the **aid** of a walking stick.

74 Zora's hotel room was large, light and very **well ventilated**.

75 Nikoli had to **amend** the last paragraph of his English essay as his teacher had discovered that he had copied it from the internet.

76 Casper always prepares a huge **variety** of sandwiches for lunch.

77 Although Kathy wasn't **averse** to Silas having his birthday party at home, she didn't really want the entire class of 30 children coming.

78 Sasha was **bewildered** by the assembly instructions for her new bookcase.

79 The goalkeeper **made a mistake** and let in a third goal.

80 Liz has a bright and **bubbly** personality.

/20

Vocabulary: matching words and their definitions

A. First, match up the words with their definitions. Write each word in the correct space.

active	constant	appalling	derelict	accurate
defective	baffled	worthwhile	curious	capable

	Word	Definition
1		beneficial
2		exactly correct
3		energetic and busy
4		horrifying/bad
5		puzzled and confused
6		able to do something
7		happening all the time and never stopping
8		eager to find something out
9		having a fault
10		neglected and in ruins

B. Now, complete the sentences using the words above.

1   Although in his 80s, Geoff still has a very _____ lifestyle.

2   Lucy is more than _____ of winning the competition.

3   Sadhil was _____ to see who his new form teacher would be.

4   Being able to speak Mandarin would be a _____ skill to have.

5   If you buy a new phone and it is _____, you can send it back and have it replaced.

6   The engineer from the gas company was _____ as to the cause of the explosion.

7   The old barn was _____ for years before they knocked it down and built a house.

8   Jibran's weather forecast turned out to be entirely _____.

9   There is _____ noise from the heavy traffic in the city centre.

10   They had to wait outside for hours in the most _____ weather.

/20

A. First, match up the words with their definitions. Write each word in the correct space.

crucial	advantageous	fatigued	content	elegant
congested	envious	courteous	fictional	biased

	Word	Definition
1		good and helpful for you
2		having a preference for one person or team more than another
3		blocked up and not allowing movement
4		happy and satisfied
5		polite and respectful
6		vital and exceedingly important
7		graceful and stylish
8		wishing you could have something that someone else has
9		extremely tired
10		made up/not real

B. Now, complete the sentences using the words above.

1 All the roads into central London are heavily _____ during the rush hour.

2 It's absolutely _____ to visit your dentist for regular check-ups.

3 Sally found that her herbal cream was extremely _____ for her skin.

4 Agata looked very _____ in her new dress.

5 Hattie arrived home feeling cold and _____ after her week-long residential trip.

6 Zain was perfectly _____ to lie in the sunshine on the beach.

7 Ava was certain that the referee was _____ towards the opposing team.

8 Bailey, tried not to show it, but he was very _____ of his brother's new bike.

9 Zara was always helpful and _____.

10 The book's author maintains that all his characters are entirely _____.

/20

A. First, match up the words with their definitions. Write each word in the correct space.

courage	appliance	achievement	bouquet	alarm
advantage	debate	assortment	donation	agony

	Word	Definition
1		a thing completed successfully
2		something that helps you or is useful to you
3		great pain or suffering
4		a sudden fear that something bad will happen
5		a machine designed to do a particular job
6		a mixture of different things
7		a bunch of flowers given to someone as a present
8		bravery or fearlessness
9		a discussion between sides with different views
10		something given, usually money, in aid of a good cause

B. Now, complete the sentences using the words above.

1   Rupert was in _____ after breaking his leg while playing rugby.

2   Jill was delighted to be given a huge _____ of tulips for her birthday.

3   Many local residents expressed _____ at the proposals for a new housing estate.

4   Dad just didn't have enough _____ to go for a ride on the rollercoaster.

5   It is a massive _____ for an athlete to win four gold medals at the Olympics.

6   Patsy was wearing a strange _____ of antique jewellery.

7   The Jones family had a heated _____ about where to go on holiday this year.

8   Emil decided to take _____ of the sunny weather and cooked on the barbecue.

9   Inaya made a very generous _____ to the charity.

10   A dishwasher is a very useful _____ to have in your kitchen.

/20

A. First, match up the words with their definitions. Write each word in the correct space.

appetite	extract	ailment	exterior	anguish
affection	encounter	ambition	fabric	adventure

	Word	**Definition**
1		an exciting experience
2		a fondness for someone or something
3		an illness, though not a serious one
4		something that you really want to do
5		a strong feeling of misery or distress
6		a desire for food
7		an unexpected meeting with someone
8		the outside of something, especially a building
9		a passage taken from a book or play or piece of music
10		material or cloth

B. Now, complete the sentences using the words above.

1 Evie's biggest _____ was to climb Mount Everest.

2 Grandad doesn't have much of an _____ these days; he eats very little.

3 Robert's trip to the Amazon rainforest was a thrilling _____.

4 The Raffles Hotel has some splendid architecture, both on the inside and on its _____.

5 Even before she became a vet, Sana always had a great _____ for all animals.

6 James was surprised to _____ his neighbour in the shop; he thought she was away.

7 Philip read an _____ from *The Hobbit* to the rest of the class.

8 Granny seems to struggle with her health; she always has some _____ or other.

9 The _____ is woven on machines in factories.

10 The death of a beloved pet can cause much _____.

/20

Making words

Circle the word that, when added to the end of the word on the left, creates a new word. Choose from the options A to D.

1

less

A	B	C	D
in	ear	on	are

2

leg

A	B	C	D
and	end	one	urn

3

dam

A	B	C	D
sun	soon	sin	son

4

he

A	B	C	D
and	address	say	essay

5

rob

A	B	C	D
on	bust	in	but

6

fore

A	B	C	D
ever	mat	go	right

7

occur

A	B	C	D
red	once	ants	rise

8

here

A	B	C	D
in	on	bye	off

9

up

A	B	C	D
less	lend	lace	lift

/9

10		A	B	C	D
	how	odd	ever	after	even

11		A	B	C	D
	fore	see	sea	rest	reign

12		A	B	C	D
	imp	ending	erring	proving	asking

13		A	B	C	D
	come	away	off	round	back

14		A	B	C	D
	arc	angel	her	chin	cave

15		A	B	C	D
	tar	turn	rise	get	gate

16		A	B	C	D
	in	pride	vent	word	get

17		A	B	C	D
	host	in	age	art	test

18		A	B	C	D
	out	went	want	word	ward

19		A	B	C	D
	flip	ant	pant	end	and

20		A	B	C	D
	over	axed	through	taste	took

/11

21

bar

A	B	C	D
row	get	gone	gin

22

had

A	B	C	D
done	deck	dine	dock

23

main

A	B	C	D
time	town	place	land

24

trait

A	B	C	D
some	less	or	tor

25

ascend

A	B	C	D
in	end	ant	at

26

tar

A	B	C	D
gate	tan	ten	tent

27

band

A	B	C	D
is	on	age	or

28

fore

A	B	C	D
ever	sight	give	get

29

over

A	B	C	D
right	run	way	back

30

pop

A	B	C	D
spies	peas	spaces	pies

/10

31		A	B	C	D
	so	at	up	or	be

32		A	B	C	D
	hum	your	are	or	an

33		A	B	C	D
	in	told	word	ward	way

34		A	B	C	D
	grate	less	fully	full	need

35		A	B	C	D
	bar	den	rid	kin	king

36		A	B	C	D
	bud	dye	dries	dies	dip

37		A	B	C	D
	trick	eye	cycle	lid	led

38		A	B	C	D
	sin	kind	kite	king	full

39		A	B	C	D
	back	log	led	word	con

40		A	B	C	D
	buoy	cot	friend	ant	led

/10

41

out

A	B	C	D
ask	pace	raid	rot

42

divers

A	B	C	D
city	urge	ion	see

43

not

A	B	C	D
thing	ace	iced	then

44

fin

A	B	C	D
any	ant	art	ally

45

post

A	B	C	D
ape	ask	age	end

46

he

A	B	C	D
at	on	up	in

47

over

A	B	C	D
along	side	way	all

48

cab

A	B	C	D
age	ice	led	lid

49

cent

A	B	C	D
red	role	roll	rule

50

am

A	B	C	D
led	lid	bled	pull

/10

Cloze passages

In the following passages, some of the words are missing. Complete each passage by selecting the words from the options A to H. Each word may only be used once. Write the correct letter in each answer lozenge.

A	B	C	D	E	F	G	H
reaches	energy	pressure	living	sources	changed	ever	present

Scientists once thought no life existed at the bottom of the sea. They knew that the water (Q1 _____) was very strong. However, that (Q2 _____) about 100 years ago. Scientists began dragging heavy nets across the sea floor. They found crabs, worms and some strange-looking fish. Total darkness begins below 900 metres. No sunlight (Q3 _____) these depths, so no plants can live there. Yet there is life in this dark world. In fact, life is (Q4 _____) in unexpected numbers and varieties. Some animals swim to the surface waters to feed. Others hunt for food in deep waters. Plant and animal remains drift down from above. These dead bodies are the main food (Q5 _____) for deep-sea life.

A	B	C	D	E	F	G	H
whatever	prey	where	elastic	under	feed	stretch	identify

Deep-sea creatures can live (Q6 _____) the water pressure is strong, and they have ways to find food in this black world. Some fish have huge mouths to help them catch anything that swims by. Others have (Q7 _____) stomachs that (Q8 _____) to hold whatever food they can find. They can eat food that is larger than they are.

Many deep-sea animals glow in the dark! They have organs that give off a brightly coloured light. The organs glow so that the animals can attract their (Q9 _____). These organs may also help fish (Q10 _____) each other and find mates.

/10

A	B	C	D	E	F	G	H
spiral	complete	naturally	whole	adhesive	bridge	entire	have

A spider's web is a truly remarkable thing. Female spiders (Q1)
produce silk, an incredibly strong, sticky substance, which they use to build their elegant,
(Q2)-shaped webs. Spiders are also highly efficient designers; they can often
complete an (Q3) web in less than an hour.

Spiders spin webs for a number of different reasons. Sometimes, a spider will spin a web to build
a (Q4) between one tree and the next. Most often, however, webs are traps
that the spider uses to capture its prey. When the spider wants to catch its dinner, it will spin a
web and then sits in its centre, waiting patiently for flies and other insects to become stuck in
the (Q5) silk.

A	B	C	D	E	F	G	H
usually	recycle	preferred	crafty	chance	employ	used	dangerous

Spiders are very sensitive to the vibrations caused by things landing in their webs. Many species
can distinguish between the vibrations caused by their (Q6) prey, like a fly,
and (Q7) insects, such as wasps.

After a while, the spider's web will start to break down and is no longer useful. At this point,
many types of spider will eat the silk, so they can (Q8) the raw material
inside their bodies, and build a new web somewhere else.

Not all spiders are web spinners, however. Many species (Q9) different
hunting strategies. Many simply chase down smaller insects on the ground. Others, such as the
(Q10) trapdoor spider, dig burrows, build a door at the entrance out of dirt
and silk and lie in wait, ready to pounce on prey when it passes by.

/10

A	B	C	D	E	F	G	H
sides	turns	timely	master	video	strategy	board	opposing

Chess is a very popular game, with countless fans across the world. The game replicates a battle between two (Q1   ) sides, represented by the white and black pieces on the chessboard. Players take (Q2   ) to make one move each, and whoever manages to 'checkmate' the opposing king is the champion.

Chess is a game of (Q3   ) and skill, and it takes years of dedicated study and practice to (Q4   ) all the best tactics and become an expert, or 'grandmaster'.

The modern game of chess is believed to have a long history. Humans have been playing (Q5   ) games for centuries, but the closest ancient version of the modern game of chess comes from India. The Indian game, chaturanga, is like chess in that two sides use a number of different pieces, including pawns, horses and elephants, to attack the other side.

A	B	C	D	E	F	G	H
south	unique	westward	minor	followed	major	adapted	version

This game became popular throughout ancient Persia, and eventually spread eastward, reaching Japan and Korea, and then later (Q6   ) to Europe. As it spread to new realms, people (Q7   ) the rules slightly. As a result, there are now many different versions, each with their own (Q8   ) aspects. The Chinese version, for example, has a 'river' in the middle of the board and only in the European (Q9   ) is there a powerful queen who can move any number of squares in any direction.

In the 20th century, chess competitions have also become more prevalent. Winners at (Q10   ) championships can walk away with hundreds of thousands of pounds in prize money.

/10

A	B	C	D	E	F	G	H
regarded	comes	competing	typically	there	mental	consists	involving

The Ironman Triathlon is widely (Q1 _____) as one of the most gruelling sporting

events in the world. It (Q2 _____) of an incredible 2.2-mile swim, followed by a

112-mile bicycle ride and then a 26.22-mile run. This means that, depending on speed and

weather conditions, athletes will (Q3 _____) need to be swimming, cycling and

running continuously for 16 hours in order just to finish.

Being able to complete in an Ironman race is a remarkable feat of physical endurance, but also

a real test of an athlete's (Q4 _____) strength. Pushing yourself so hard can even

be dangerous to your health. Because of this, athletes considering (Q5 _____) in a

triathlon should undergo a full medical check-up before they start their training.

A	B	C	D	E	F	G	H
athlete	prominence	novice	driven	practice	soft	ferocious	future

The first Ironman event was held in 1978 in Hawaii, meaning that on top of everything else,

athletes also had to deal with the (Q6 _____) heat. Today, there are more than

70 Ironman competitions held annually all over the globe, although the Hawaii one remains the

most prestigious. Experts say that a (Q7 _____) will need around a year of serious

dedication to train for an Ironman race, although in (Q8 _____), probably much

longer.

Anyone over 18 can apply to compete in an Ironman, and some particularly (Q9 _____)

athletes have completed the course in under eight hours. In 2018, Hiromu Inada from Japan

came to (Q10 _____) as the oldest person to ever complete an Ironman triathlon,

crossing the finish line in just under 17 hours. His accomplishment is even more notable

when you learn that he only completed his first triathlon at the age of 70!

/10

A	B	C	D	E	F	G	H
omen	opinions	assist	disturb	allies	enemies	treated	thought

Do cats bring good luck or bad luck? Today, (Q1_____) differ. In most of the world, for most of history, cats have been looked on with affection and honour. In the Far East, Thai legends tell of cats guarding temples. In Japan, in the 11th century, the palace kittens were (Q2_____) as princes, and it is even said that the Prophet Muhammad once cut one of the sleeves off his robe rather than (Q3_____) his sleeping cat.

Only in medieval Europe was the cat regarded as an evil (Q4_____) and associated with witchcraft.

For thousands of years, humankind's greatest (Q5_____) were neither wolves nor snakes, but the mice that ate food stores and spread diseases. The early Egyptians noticed wild cats hunting mice, so they encouraged and tamed them.

A	B	C	D	E	F	G	H
catch	square	revered	crescent	initially	lineage	descendants	realised

The Egyptians (Q6_____) that as well as being useful for controlling pests, cats were also beautiful and very maternal animals. Cats were loved for these qualities in people's homes, and in temples they were (Q7_____) as sacred beings.

Cats were (Q8_____) said to belong to the Sun God, but then later became associated with goddesses and with the moon. Like the moon, a cat's eyes glow in the dark, and their pupils can assume different shapes, changing from round to a (Q9_____) shape and back again.

The Egyptians were the first humans to successfully tame wild cats. Every modern house cat can trace its (Q10_____) back to ancient Egypt; the Greeks transported them from Africa to Europe, and from there they travelled by ship to most countries in the world.

/10

A	B	C	D	E	F	G	H
wed	home	resided	scorching	leaving	chores	watering	grateful

The legend of Chang'e and Hou Yi is famous in Chinese folklore. Chang'e was a beautiful young fairy who (Q1_____) in the Jade palace, in heaven. One day, while going about her (Q2_____) in the palace, Chang'e accidentally smashed a vase. In fury, the Emperor banished Chang'e from heaven, and sent her to live on Earth. While on Earth, Chang'e met Hou Yi, an expert archer. They fell in love and were (Q3_____). One day a terrible thing happened. Ten suns rose in the sky one morning. They beat down on the earth, (Q4_____) the crops and drying up the wells. Luckily, Hou Yi stepped forward with his bow and arrow and shot down the extra nine suns. The people were so (Q5_____) to Hou Yi, they venerated him as a hero, and he became king, with Chang'e as his queen.

A	B	C	D	E	F	G	H
plunged	evermore	represent	kindly	harshly	floated	crept	once

But King Hou Yi turned out to be an evil king, who ruled (Q6_____). He ruled over the Earth for many years. But King Hou Yi was growing older. He ordered his palace sages to create an elixir of life, so that he could make himself immortal, and continue his reign of terror over the Earth for (Q7_____). Chang'e knew that Hou Yi had become an evil king. So, when the sages finished making the elixir, Chang'e (Q8_____) into their room, stole the elixir and swallowed it herself! Hou Yi tried to kill her, but Chang'e fled by leaping from a high window. But since Chang'e was really a fairy rather than a human, instead of falling, she (Q9_____) upwards into the sky and landed on the moon. She remains there to this day. The Chinese say, if you look closely enough at the moon, you can still catch a glimpse of her. And so it was that Chang'e and Hou Yi came to (Q10_____) the moon and the sun, the yin and the yang.

/10

Shuffled sentences

In each question below, the words may be rearranged to form a sentence. One word does not belong in the sentence. Circle the superfluous word from the options A to H.

1

interfere	signals	frequent	hills	with	often	can	radio
A	B	C	D	E	F	G	H

2

leaping	to	Australia	kangaroos	jump	mammals	are	native
A	B	C	D	E	F	G	H

3

made	is	a	from	tomatoes	sauce	brown	ketchup
A	B	C	D	E	F	G	H

4

in	were	the	zoo	there	dense	tigers	jungle
A	B	C	D	E	F	G	H

5

lodged	the	Dhiya	annoyed	complaint	with	council	a
A	B	C	D	E	F	G	H

6

roast	cooks	Sunday	every	lunch	Amy	means	a
A	B	C	D	E	F	G	H

7

stop	jolted	station	the	sudden	to	train	a
A	B	C	D	E	F	G	H

8

several	from	souvenirs	Sonia	Spain	brought	back	flew
A	B	C	D	E	F	G	H

/8

9

slow	an	Raj	and	methodical	was	worker	a
A	B	C	D	E	F	G	H

10

has	party	every	afternoon	piano	Mahin	Thursday	lessons
A	B	C	D	E	F	G	H

11

next	in	line	the	nobody	door	lives	house
A	B	C	D	E	F	G	H

12

to	boys	any	dangers	oblivious	were	strange	the
A	B	C	D	E	F	G	H

13

he	forgotten	Lucas	passport	his	sad	realised	had
A	B	C	D	E	F	G	H

14

car	drives	my	that	joy	and	is	pride
A	B	C	D	E	F	G	H

15

five	range	to	ten	prices	pounds	from	costs
A	B	C	D	E	F	G	H

16

together	the	exploded	broken	with	stick	pieces	glue
A	B	C	D	E	F	G	H

17

both	and	instruments	wind	flutes	blow	are	saxophones
A	B	C	D	E	F	G	H

18

wound	neck	a	around	tangle	Vidhya	her	scarf
A	B	C	D	E	F	G	H

19

longer	fruit	in	bananas	usually	the	fridge	keeps
A	B	C	D	E	F	G	H

/11

20

himself	Stefan	drinks	a	glass	poured	milk	of
A	B	C	D	E	F	G	H

21

he	ride	bike	Ben	washed	whistled	his	as
A	B	C	D	E	F	G	H

22

set	northerly	a	off	upon	in	direction	Marie
A	B	C	D	E	F	G	H

23

been	well	Joshua	lately	has	too	feels	not
A	B	C	D	E	F	G	H

24

dough	divided	into	kept	Daria	four	the	pieces
A	B	C	D	E	F	G	H

25

fire	tested	week	the	alarm	every	is	loud
A	B	C	D	E	F	G	H

26

simple	Arushi	a	red	was	as	wearing	dress
A	B	C	D	E	F	G	H

27

was	to	snow	the	cancelled	light	due	game
A	B	C	D	E	F	G	H

28

car	Joe	with	water	away	washed	soapy	his
A	B	C	D	E	F	G	H

29

doctor	the	waiting	kept	ages	for	Mia	bored
A	B	C	D	E	F	G	H

30

uploaded	his	of	Ravi	a	kittens	very	video
A	B	C	D	E	F	G	H

/11

31

was	remember	struggling	ask	Maisie	her	to	password
A	B	C	D	E	F	G	H

32

presents	Aaryan	birthday	many	times	his	on	unwrapped
A	B	C	D	E	F	G	H

33

unexpected	a	the	winning	was	surprise	an	competition
A	B	C	D	E	F	G	H

34

undeniably	playing	net	Surita	at	is	good	tennis
A	B	C	D	E	F	G	H

35

and	the	lounge	around	Arushi	twirled	danced	when
A	B	C	D	E	F	G	H

36

her	branch	Tansy	a	elbow	pain	grazed	on
A	B	C	D	E	F	G	H

37

an	dinosaurs	Gus	of	has	encyclopaedic	lot	knowledge
A	B	C	D	E	F	G	H

38

her	long	Jodie	for	asked	a	trim	hairdresser
A	B	C	D	E	F	G	H

39

gathered	tree	we	shade	under	for	heat	a
A	B	C	D	E	F	G	H

40

to	singer	be	a	Kiana	opera	an	wants
A	B	C	D	E	F	G	H

/10

41

in	brother	longer	my	his	is	thirties	now
A	B	C	D	E	F	G	H

42

been	things	lately	going	well	have	extremely	every
A	B	C	D	E	F	G	H

43

desk	room	too	the	much	took	office	up
A	B	C	D	E	F	G	H

44

wanted	up	marrying	childhood	ended	Sienna	sweetheart	her
A	B	C	D	E	F	G	H

45

me	taking	her	Sally	for	travelling	home	thanked
A	B	C	D	E	F	G	H

46

some	just	terrible	went	Mohan	news	received	had
A	B	C	D	E	F	G	H

47

was	before	feeling	interview	prior	nervous	his	Bhupen
A	B	C	D	E	F	G	H

48

flapped	newspaper	Millie	with	fly	swatted	the	a
A	B	C	D	E	F	G	H

49

struggled	assemble	bookcase	his	Adrian	new	to	gather
A	B	C	D	E	F	G	H

50

course	dine	the	was	roasted	a	main	chicken
A	B	C	D	E	F	G	H

/10

51

were	mystery	stumped	virus	the	scientists	by	source
A	B	C	D	E	F	G	H

52

stayed	could	movie	up	the	we	watching	late
A	B	C	D	E	F	G	H

53

exam	stapled	the	together	all	papers	collect	Henry
A	B	C	D	E	F	G	H

54

diamond	was	expensive	a	Kate	necklace	wearing	an
A	B	C	D	E	F	G	H

55

painting	the	an	hung	wall	on	a	framed
A	B	C	D	E	F	G	H

56

stadium	of	into	packed	fans	band	the	thousands
A	B	C	D	E	F	G	H

57

pasta	salad	Swati	bill	and	mixed	a	ordered
A	B	C	D	E	F	G	H

58

wicked	has	sense	a	Aria	humour	of	at
A	B	C	D	E	F	G	H

59

riding	school	gates	Trisha	to	loves	her	bicycle
A	B	C	D	E	F	G	H

60

at	on	they	photo	laughed	and	looked	the
A	B	C	D	E	F	G	H

/10

Answers

	Spelling pp.5–6	
1	C	lenient
2	B	spicy
3	A	principal
4	A	savoured
5	B	through
6	C	whose
7	B	minor
8	C	role
9	A	razed
10	B	plain
11	N	–
12	A	muscles
13	C	conscious
14	A	curiosity
15	D	lessons
16	D	committee
17	D	forty
18	D	weird
19	C	boarding
20	D	beach
21	D	alterations
22	D	review
23	B	leisure
24	A	truly
25	C	unfamiliar
26	N	–
27	C	ceiling
28	B	palette
29	B	hoarse

	Spelling pp.7–8	
30	A	wrung
31	D	gist
32	B	source
33	N	–
34	C	independent
35	C	advice
36	C	definitely
37	C	desserts
38	A	vain
39	C	hangers
40	N	–
41	B	neigh
42	B	pale
43	B	kerb
44	D	mousse
45	B	fleas
46	D	irresistible
47	C	lollipop
48	N	–
49	B	embarrassed
50	B	noticeable
51	D	persistent
52	D	draught
53	C	profit
54	B	pedals
55	A	allowed
56	B	harassed
57	B	threshold
58	B	religious
59	N	–
60	A	unforeseen

	Synonyms p.9
1	protected
2	impartial
3	vulgar
4	pamper
5	inform
6	liable
7	related
8	exhausted
9	cheerfully
10	jealousy
11	astound
12	jittery
13	expired
14	largely
15	suspicious
16	temporary
17	impressive
18	affection
19	volatile
20	livid
21	grim
22	ruled
23	loyal

	Synonyms p.10
24	merge
25	mindful
26	incredible
27	diary
28	recently
29	locate
30	diminutive
31	injure
32	comprehend
33	adjust
34	method
35	motivate
36	dappled
37	murky
38	initial
39	rebellion
40	mystify
41	negotiate
42	dampness
43	ordinarily
44	novice
45	invalid
46	inflexible
47	obscure
48	obstacle
49	occurrence

Answers

Synonyms p.11		Synonyms p.12		Antonyms p.13		Antonyms p.14	
50	curiously	76	mirth	1	intact	24	unconcerned
51	intersection	77	outline	2	separate	25	denial
52	ordinary	78	competitor	3	lenient	26	anonymous
53	mariner	79	pointless	4	liberty	27	approval
54	odious	80	contaminate	5	kind	28	outdated
55	odourless	81	ration	6	agitate	29	simplicity
56	ominous	82	sure	7	unknown	30	consent
57	exclude	83	perilous	8	oppose	31	console
58	vitality	84	wait	9	natural	32	helpful
59	viewpoint	85	precise	10	generous	33	dawdle
60	systematic	86	forecast	11	upright	34	inexpensive
61	outsmart	87	prefer	12	veteran	35	deceitfully
62	overbearing	88	missing	13	gradually	36	decipher
63	supervise	89	valuable	14	abstain	37	dedicated
64	splendid	90	purchase	15	reasonable	38	deduction
65	procession	91	propel	16	rejection	39	graceful
66	enigma	92	outspoken	17	inaccurate	40	displeasure
67	partial	93	progress	18	reassuring	41	deliberate
68	specific	94	evidence	19	irksome	42	insult
69	enduring	95	overcome	20	ashamed	43	return
70	convincing	96	likely	21	contempt	44	prosperous
71	calmly	97	prosperity	22	compassion	45	provide
72	plea	98	pry	23	compelling	46	despair
73	dilemma	99	presently			47	creation
74	overdue	100	strict			48	improve
75	swoop					49	deter

Answers

Antonyms
p.15

50	healthy
51	assertive
52	dingy
53	cleanse
54	emerge
55	detached
56	receive
57	disclose
58	courteous
59	disloyal
60	displeased
61	unify
62	unlikely
63	drain
64	demanding
65	wasteful
66	elevate
67	clarify
68	protect
69	endless
70	energetic
71	enlightened
72	roughly
73	squander
74	unskilled
75	extract

Antonyms
p.16

76	moderate
77	forged
78	powerful
79	drought
80	previous
81	forlorn
82	stale
83	unwilling
84	specific
85	disagreeable
86	blustery
87	retain
88	uncertain
89	boisterous
90	unfasten
91	fantasy
92	humid
93	probable
94	methodical
95	suitable
96	complicated
97	changeable
98	unnecessary
99	unofficial
100	exclude

Synonyms: missing letters
pp.17–18

1	flawless
2	immense
3	inventive
4	stunning
5	estimate
6	amazing
7	tempest
8	instinct
9	triumph
10	suitable
11	startled
12	doubtful
13	banned
14	tedious
15	final
16	appalling
17	thorough
18	thriving
19	irritating
20	bearable
21	tremble
22	absence
23	turbulent
24	gratitude
25	invincible
26	believable
27	uncertain
28	persuade
29	utterly

Synonyms: missing letters
pp.19–20

30	conquer
31	assorted
32	vastly
33	savage
34	voyage
35	withdraw
36	shabby
37	roughly
38	abruptly
39	adjust
40	obtain
41	adhere
42	critical
43	confessed
44	adorable
45	altitude
46	quantity
47	additional
48	applaud
49	fitting
50	difficult
51	fragrance
52	achieve
53	drenched
54	awkward
55	support
56	bewilder
57	benefit
58	beside
59	broaden
60	changeable

Answers

Antonyms: missing letters pp.21–22

1	impress
2	adequate
3	competent
4	install
5	abolish
6	separate
7	visible
8	miserable
9	reluctant
10	strenuous
11	hurried
12	lethal
13	flimsy
14	scarcely
15	rapidly
16	rashly
17	quality
18	rebuild
19	advance
20	improve
21	attract
22	resist
23	pleasant
24	gripping
25	exact
26	natural
27	wisdom
28	salvage
29	identical

Antonyms: missing letters pp.23–24

30	expenses
31	confident
32	critical
33	complete
34	secretive
35	release
36	sensible
37	together
38	jagged
39	severe
40	superior
41	trivial
42	silent
43	harmless
44	coarse
45	friendly
46	praise
47	spacious
48	spiteful
49	inactive
50	standard
51	starve
52	stationary
53	steeply
54	unclean
55	inspire
56	terminate
57	stubborn
58	submerge
59	increase
60	sweltering

Synonyms: the odd one out p.25

1	attention
2	diary
3	vague
4	special
5	collector
6	genuine
7	habitat
8	brawl
9	cursory
10	ominous
11	tangle
12	replay
13	astute
14	fractured
15	distribution
16	wallow
17	thoughtful
18	baleful
19	change
20	orderly
21	report
22	linear
23	solidarity

Synonyms: the odd one out p.26

24	abashed
25	acute
26	prevention
27	select
28	jealousy
29	wander
30	equal
31	twitter
32	rebel
33	obtuse
34	ban
35	perform
36	shrill
37	strike
38	explore
39	trial
40	disrupt
41	bowl
42	modify
43	scold
44	opponent
45	hedge
46	exceed
47	squander
48	variety
49	credulous

Answers

	Synonyms: the odd one out p.27		Synonyms: the odd one out p.28		Vocabulary revision p.29		Vocabulary revision p.30

	Synonyms: the odd one out p.27
50	rhombus
51	incomplete
52	remorse
53	immunity
54	memorise
55	modest
56	devise
57	convenience
58	split
59	spray
60	part
61	serious
62	rhyme
63	scribble
64	scarcely
65	stark
66	engage
67	shady
68	promote
69	present
70	trample
71	ensnare
72	prim
73	discussion
74	vista
75	push

	Synonyms: the odd one out p.28
76	flutter
77	brake
78	customer
79	summary
80	agility
81	obedient
82	luxury
83	worldly
84	carnage
85	concerned
86	charge
87	care
88	baffled
89	enrich
90	inevitable
91	award
92	sly
93	gruesome
94	slide
95	peculiar
96	bustle
97	splash
98	grateful
99	reserve
100	gruelling

	Vocabulary revision p.29	
1	O	survivors
2	F	decided
3	I	fit
4	C	opening
5	T	illustrate
6	L	ignore
7	A	imagine
8	J	innocent
9	H	investigate
10	Q	exhausted
11	M	tolerant
12	P	resemble
13	R	manage
14	E	obedient
15	D	monitor
16	N	oppose
17	B	perfect
18	K	location
19	G	overjoyed
20	S	certain

	Vocabulary revision p.30	
21	C	practical
22	N	sufficient
23	Q	withered
24	E	saturated
25	L	vacant
26	D	disorganised
27	T	valuable
28	G	unemployed
29	M	grotesque
30	J	rotate
31	A	forgetful
32	H	accustomed to
33	S	ambition
34	P	naive
35	I	novelist
36	B	unwell
37	K	outrun
38	F	shocked
39	R	thirsty
40	O	speechless

Answers

	Vocabulary revision p.31		Vocabulary revision p.32		Vocabulary: matching words and their definitions p.33		Vocabulary: matching words and their definitions p.34

Vocabulary revision p.31

41	J	monitoring
42	Q	improving
43	C	conceal
44	H	arrogant
45	A	nimble
46	T	ajar
47	F	leave
48	O	modify
49	L	entry
50	B	afford
51	M	always
52	E	blonde
53	S	cheap
54	P	choice
55	D	concentrate
56	K	dusting
57	I	criticise
58	G	dare
59	R	discovered
60	N	miserable

Vocabulary revision p.32

61	K	remain
62	B	honest
63	Q	undecided
64	P	accelerate
65	I	authorise
66	F	crucial
67	N	answer
68	D	unenthusiastic
69	R	cosy
70	T	toxic
71	M	omit
72	G	lovable
73	O	assistance
74	A	airy
75	H	alter
76	L	assortment
77	S	opposed
78	E	baffled
79	C	blundered
80	J	sparkling

Vocabulary: matching words and their definitions p.33

A

1	worthwhile
2	accurate
3	active
4	appalling
5	baffled
6	capable
7	constant
8	curious
9	defective
10	derelict

B

1	active
2	capable
3	curious
4	worthwhile
5	defective
6	baffled
7	derelict
8	accurate
9	constant
10	appalling

Vocabulary: matching words and their definitions p.34

A

1	advantageous
2	biased
3	congested
4	content
5	courteous
6	crucial
7	elegant
8	envious
9	fatigued
10	fictional

B

1	congested
2	crucial
3	advatageous
4	elegant
5	fatigued
6	content
7	biased
8	envious
9	courteous
10	fictional

Answers

Vocabulary: matching words and their definitions
p.35

A	
1	achievement
2	advantage
3	agony
4	alarm
5	appliance
6	assortment
7	bouquet
8	courage
9	debate
10	donation

B	
1	agony
2	bouquet
3	alarm
4	courage
5	achievement
6	assortment
7	debate
8	advantage
9	donation
10	appliance

Vocabulary: matching words and their definitions
p.36

A	
1	adventure
2	affection
3	ailment
4	ambition
5	anguish
6	appetite
7	encounter
8	exterior
9	extract
10	fabric

B	
1	ambition
2	appetite
3	adventure
4	exterior
5	affection
6	encounter
7	extract
8	ailment
9	fabric
10	anguish

Making words
pp.37–39

1	C	lesson
2	B	legend
3	D	damson
4	B	headdress
5	C	robin
6	C	forego
7	A	occurred
8	A	herein
9	D	uplift
10	B	however
11	A	foresee
12	A	impending
13	D	comeback
14	B	archer
15	C	target
16	B	invent
17	B	hostage
18	D	outward
19	B	flippant
20	D	overtook
21	A	barrow
22	D	haddock
23	D	mainland
24	C	traitor
25	C	ascendant
26	B	tartan
27	C	bandage
28	B	foresight
29	B	overrun
30	D	poppies

Making words
pp.40–41

31	B	soup
32	D	human
33	C	inward
34	B	gratefully
35	D	barking
36	C	buddies
37	D	trickled
38	C	sinking
39	A	backlog
40	C	buoyant
41	B	outpace
42	C	diversion
43	C	noticed
44	D	finally
45	C	postage
46	A	heat
47	D	overall
48	C	cabled
49	A	centred
50	C	ambled

Answers

Cloze passages
p.42

1	C	pressure
2	F	changed
3	A	reaches
4	H	present
5	E	sources
6	C	where
7	D	elastic
8	G	stretch
9	B	prey
10	H	identify

Cloze passages
p.43

1	C	naturally
2	A	spiral
3	G	entire
4	F	bridge
5	E	adhesive
6	C	preferred
7	H	dangerous
8	B	recycle
9	F	employ
10	D	crafty

Cloze passages
p.44

1	H	opposing
2	B	turns
3	F	strategy
4	D	master
5	G	board
6	C	westward
7	G	adapted
8	B	unique
9	H	version
10	F	major

Cloze passages
p.45

1	A	regarded
2	G	consists
3	D	typically
4	F	mental
5	C	competing
6	G	ferocious
7	C	novice
8	E	practice
9	D	driven
10	B	prominence

Cloze passages
p.46

1	B	opinions
2	G	treated
3	D	disturb
4	A	omen
5	F	enemies
6	H	realised
7	C	revered
8	E	initially
9	D	crescent
10	F	lineage

Cloze passages
p.47

1	C	resided
2	F	chores
3	A	wed
4	D	scorching
5	H	grateful
6	E	harshly
7	B	evermore
8	G	crept
9	F	floated
10	C	represent

Shuffled sentences
pp.48–50

1	C
2	E
3	G
4	D
5	D
6	G
7	C
8	H
9	B
10	B
11	C
12	G
13	F
14	B
15	H
16	C
17	F
18	E
19	D
20	C
21	B
22	E
23	G
24	D
25	H
26	F
27	F
28	E
29	H
30	G

Shuffled sentences
pp.51–53

31	D
32	E
33	B
34	C
35	H
36	F
37	G
38	B
39	G
40	D
41	C
42	H
43	G
44	A
45	F
46	D
47	E
48	A
49	H
50	B
51	H
52	B
53	G
54	D
55	C
56	F
57	D
58	H
59	C
60	B

Notes

Notes